Dr. Om___ _____ ____ ____ the impact of war and
dislocati
about e_____ _____ _____
from surviv_rs on how to cope with everyday life. It is
impressive, not only in its scientific content, but also in
its presentation. It is a poetical essay that highlights the
importance of love and hope in our lives and in the care
of children. These ideas are expressed in the metaphor
of *Untangled* and in its mantra for families to recite, "This
is us, together." Dr. Reda brings to us beautiful ideas and
images that can help us protect and heal our children, our
families, and our communities affected by trauma. Thank
you, Dr. Reda, for this excellent contribution.

Dr. Richard F. Mollica, MD, MAR

Professor of Psychiatry, Harvard Medical School

In this book, Dr. Omar Reda offers a deeply compassionate exploration of trauma-informed parenting. His
heartfelt dedication to improving the lives of children and
families stands out on every page. Dr. Reda understands
the needs of both parents and children, and he shares
openly from his own parenting experience. The drawings
from children are a beautiful touch. This book can have a
powerful impact to improve the lives of people who have
suffered and who can heal.

Lisa Najavits, PhD

Director of Treatment Innovations and adjunct professor
at University of Massachusetts Medical School

D0745728

Dr. Omar Reda's work is deeply compassionate, intelligent, and thoughtful. *Untangled* is a needed book that has the capacity to change the world one life at a time. By drawing on research and his extensive experience, both personal and professional, Dr. Reda has found the words that give voice to traumatized children and their families. *Untangled* is respectful, practical, and most importantly, hopeful. In his own words, because they are so powerful, "Trauma loses its power to ruin us when love and hope step in." *Untangled* is this step in.

Karen Young

Author, speaker, and psychotherapist,
specializing in childhood and adolescent anxiety

Trauma is one of the most impactful, isolating, and developmentally disrupting experiences humans face. It tears down, it injures, and its effects spread like a cancer when left unexplored. Dr. Omar Reda knows this and refuses to let this be.

In his groundbreaking book, *Untangled*, Dr. Reda gives parents and families the information and tools they need to address and work through individual and cultural trauma while, at the same time, offering a strong example of how to do so with his authoritative, yet deeply loving, voice. This is far more than a workbook. It is a guidebook, offering descriptions of what trauma is and how it impacts families and children in a language that is accessible to all. Guided explorative questions and surveys peppered throughout the book offer opportunities for reflection and application as well as planning and goal setting.

For parents facing the daunting task of helping their children navigate traumatic experiences well, this is an indescribable gift. Dr. Reda wisely says, "The truth is, trauma has entered your family. There is no getting around it, but there are ways through it. You and your family have more to untangle than families who have not been terrorized by trauma, and you may feel, at times, like healing is impossible or out of reach." From here he offers all the wisdom possible into the reaching hands of those who suffer.

I am a psychologist and yet, when my own family suffered a traumatic loss, I felt adrift and untethered, uncertain of how to help my children live through indescribable grief while I, myself, was also suffering. I wish a book like *Untangled* would have been available to me at that time. This book is part comfort, part authoritative guide, and wholly grounding.

If someone you love has experienced trauma, please read this book, take notes, use the worksheets, then go and put all you've learned into practice. In this way we could heal the world.

Doreen Dodgen-Magee, Psy.D.

Cinical Psychologist and author of
Deviced! Balancing Life and Technology in a Digital World

Untangled

A Go-To Guide for Caregivers of Traumatized
Children, Families, and Communities

Omar Reda, MD

chehalem press

Untangled

A Go-To Guide for Caregivers of Traumatized
Children, Families, and Communities

©2019 by Omar Reda, MD

Chehalem Press
Newberg, Oregon
www.chehalempress.com

Printed in the United States of America

Book art consists of hand-painted images by survivors of different types of
trauma, including Syrian refugee children.

Interior and cover design: Mareesa Fawver Moss

Book Development Editor: Jan Black

Editorial Assistant: Gracie Schafer

ISBN 978-1-59498-059-6

Message to the Reader

If you are a parent or caregiver whose children have been traumatized by events like war, forced displacement, disaster, abuse, neglect, or violence, I have written this book for you.

I want to reassure you that you have the power to set the stage for your children to heal, and to be the strong, loving advocate you want to be and that they need you to be.

This book will increase your understanding about your empowering role, what your children need, how they develop, how trauma interrupts their development, how to show your children healing love and attention, and how to use community resources to achieve that. It will also suggest ways to take care of yourself in the process.

I became a psychiatrist in 2009 and have seen thousands of clients with different mental health diagnoses in all kinds of settings—inpatient, outpatient, civil, and forensic. I have worked with male and female children, adolescents, adults, and the elderly, both in the USA and abroad, including war and disaster-affected societies.

I have experienced trauma myself as an asylum seeker.

One heart-breaking theme I have found to be all too common is that the symptoms and "disorders" found in many traumatized children stem from interpersonal dynamics and not just from genetics—a combination of nature and nurture if you like. Therefore, many are potentially preventable. This also means that if the trauma has already happened, we as parents, caregivers, and professionals working with youth can intervene to create favorable outcomes before it is too late.

Trauma causes substantial pain and suffering and can inevitably create cycles of dysfunction that may span generations. We can and should break these cycles and build bridges of trust and empowerment that renew hope and help families heal, not just for this generation but for the sake of all those to follow.

The good news is that children are resilient and have innate abilities to recover from their painful past, heal the invisible wounds of trauma, and rebuild their lives. But this will not occur without the perseverance and hard work of good people who care deeply about children.

If you are a mental health professional, a teacher, an advocate, or community leader, I have also written this book with you in mind. This guide can be a helpful resource to recommend or gift to your clients and community members.

This is mainly a book about hope. It is through the safe and genuine expression of love that we can support the physical, emotional, and spiritual well-being of our children, and ensure peace for future generations. **Love is the very definition of healing**.

As parents, caregivers, and community leaders, we can use the power of our human connections to build bridges of trust and open channels of communication with our children in ways that can prevent or reduce the effects of trauma and steer young generations toward a more positive and empowering future.

This is what I aspire to do for my children, and I invite you to aspire to do the same for yours. It is my wish that you will find what I have written helpful in doing that.

This is a flexible guide. There is no one size that fits all. Modify it as you see best for your family's unique spirit, needs, and dynamics. Make sure you take care of you too by building a community of support.

It takes a village to heal a child.

I welcome your feedback, thoughts, and suggestions at omar@projectuntangled.org

Omar Reda, MD
Portland, Oregon
2019

Contents

UNTANGLED

WE ARE CHILDREN BRAVING TRAUMA
Beautiful souls whose faith in a safe world
has been shaken but not lost,
Tossed, but standing,
See our resilience, feel our spirit, watch us flourish.
We weave a new story, Hope's glory.

WE ARE FAMILIES OVERCOMING TRAUMA
Resilient beings bonded by times of distress and delight,
We light our way,
Skilled in healing, unconditional and accepting.
Safe and at ease, Hope sees.

WE ARE PARENTS OUTSMARTING TRAUMA,
Unstoppable guardians of our children's future well-being,
Freeing the tangled,
Igniting courage to take on the world.
Trauma steals, Hope heals.

An excerpt from Untangled ~ A Go-To Guide for Parents and
Caregivers of Traumatized Children by Dr. Omar Reda.
ProjectUntangled.org. Art and design by Jan Black. Heart image by Syrian Refugee Child.

PART 1: TRAUMA, HOPE, AND HEALING LOVE

TRAUMA HAS VISITED US,
and Love and Hope will heal and sustain us.

Part 1:
Trauma, Hope, and Healing Love

Love and hope can heal us from trauma. I see it every day in my practice and in my work with traumatized families in my immediate community and in many others around the world.

Trauma loses its power to ruin us when love and hope step in.

> Trauma terrifies; love and hope comfort and inspire.
>
> Trauma destroys; love and hope rebuild.
>
> Trauma robs; love and hope restore.
>
> Trauma separates; love and hope unite.
>
> Trauma breaks hearts; love and hope mend them.
>
> Trauma leaves scars; love and hope tend them.
>
> Trauma revisits; love and hope protect.

Let's look at what trauma is, and also remind ourselves about love and hope.

Trauma

In this beautiful world there is trauma. What turns a stressful event into a traumatic one? It is the intense feeling that your life or safety, or the life or safety of a loved one, is in imminent, unescapable danger or that you are no longer in control.

There are many kinds of trauma, and I have listed some of them here for you so you can be clear in your own mind and specific with others when needed.

The National Child Traumatic Stress Network (nctsn.org) sorts trauma into these categories:

- Community violence: Exposure to intentional acts of interpersonal violence committed in public areas by individuals who are not intimately related to the victim. One unfortunate common example we see these days is the random indiscriminate killing of civilians, like in war zones or as is the case in school shootings.

- Complex trauma: Exposure to multiple traumatic events—often of an invasive, interpersonal nature—and the wide-ranging, long-term effects of this exposure.

- Disasters: Natural disasters, such as hurricanes, earthquakes, tornadoes, wildfires, tsunamis, and floods, as well as extreme weather events such as blizzards, droughts, extreme heat, and wind storms.

- Domestic violence: When an individual in the home purposely causes harm or threatens the risk of harm to a past or current partner, spouse, or family member.

- Early childhood trauma: Traumatic experiences that occur to children.

- Medical trauma: A set of psychological and physiological responses of children and their families to single or multiple medical events.

- Child physical abuse: A parent or caregiver commits an act that results in physical injury to a child or adolescent.

- Refugee trauma: Trauma related to war or persecution that may affect the mental and physical health of families long after the events have occurred. This type of trauma layers upon other traumas, such as forced displacement, seeking asylum, and leaving home.

- Child sexual abuse: Any interaction between a child and an adult (or another child) in which the child is used for the sexual stimulation of the perpetrator or an observer. This is usually about ascertaining control, not about the sexual act itself. Sometimes, sexual trauma can happen in the family context as in the case of incest.

- Terrorism and violence: Mass violence, acts of terrorism, or community trauma in the form of shootings, bombings, kidnapping, hijacking, or other types of attacks, often committed to advance a certain ideology or promote a political or religious agenda.

- Traumatic grief: Ongoing difficulties over the death or loss of someone that interfere with everyday life and make it difficult to recall positive memories of loved ones.

- Intimate interpersonal violence, such as torture, sexual assault, and incest. This type of trauma often deeply affects survivors, many of whom internalize the unwanted touch and turn the experience into self-blame.

Trauma can happen once, as in an earthquake or car accident, or over and over, as in war zones or abusive homes. Staying alive is a daily struggle for many, including children. It can be difficult for families to give children the sensitive care they need and deserve without help and education, which is why many mental health professionals and volunteers around the world are hurrying to give assistance and information to traumatized children and families.

What trauma has affected your family or those in your care? Look at the list below and check the type(s) of trauma that members of your family have experienced. This is your mountain of healing to climb, together, with others ready to help you.

- ☐ Community violence
- ☐ Complex trauma
- ☐ Disasters
- ☐ Domestic violence
- ☐ Early childhood trauma
- ☐ Medical trauma
- ☐ Physical abuse
- ☐ Refugee trauma
- ☐ Sexual abuse
- ☐ Terrorism
- ☐ Traumatic grief
- ☐ Intimate interpersonal violence

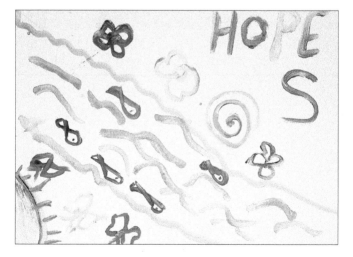

PART 2: CHILDREN

WE ARE CHILDREN BRAVING TRAUMA
Beautiful souls whose faith in a safe world
has been shaken but not lost,
Tossed, but standing.
See our resilience, feel our spirit, watch us flourish.
We weave a new story, Hope's glory.

Part 2: Children

Let's begin with the children.

Children are beautiful, perfect-the-way-they-are individuals, full of energy and the desire to imagine, wander, and explore, with the potential to blossom. They are delightful beings worthy of safe upbringing, unlimited opportunities, and unconditional love in order to meet the full possibilities of who they were created to be.

Children Are

- beautiful as they are;
- young human beings;
- dependent on others to survive;
- full of passion, unlimited potential, talent, intelligence, personality, thoughts, hopes, and feelings;
- playful and curious;
- eager learners;
- products of their parents, but not possessions;
- easily shaped and influenced;
- in need of basic needs, physical and emotional safety, and loving presence.

Children of Trauma

Children of trauma are children who have been unfairly subjected to experiences that have shaken their core values and fundamental beliefs in a safe world where humanity and beauty should have been the norm and where adults should have been trusted.

It is important to not label these children but rather weave their trauma story in ways that help them emerge from that painful ordeal unscathed, wholesome, and holy.

Children of Trauma Are

- beautiful as they are—with new reasons to doubt their beauty;
- young human beings—who have encountered at least one natural or man-made traumatic experience such as abuse, neglect, violence, war, forced displacement, or relocation;
- dependent on others to survive—and heal from the trauma;
- full of passion, unlimited potential, talent, intelligence, personality, thoughts, hopes, and feelings—as well as new worries, disturbing memories, and unsettling terrors;
- playful and curious—and at times playful in ways that reenact the traumatic theme;
- eager learners—though often distracted by concerns, memories, and anxieties;
- products of their parents, but not possessions—and now also products of trauma;

- easily shaped and influenced—but usually less easily able to trust;
- in need of basic needs, physical and emotional safety, loving presence—as well as patience and understanding.

What Children Need

Children need emotionally-engaged parents/caregivers who can keep eye contact and provide a genuine smile, a caring touch, warm hugs, kisses, and when needed, a shoulder to cry on.

Children first need to have their basic needs met, because otherwise it is not easy to give what you have not received, and it is exhausting to keep running on an empty tank.

As loving parents or caregivers, we want to give our children what they most need to feel good about themselves and the world in spite of the trauma they have encountered. When you understand what your child needs, you are better able to supply it for them. This makes life better for all of you because they receive what they need, and your desire to parent well is fulfilled.

I like to say, "We nourish so they can flourish."

The word "nourish" means to tend, to supply what is needed to grow. We nourish our children by giving them what they need to grow. By this I don't only mean the material and physical wants, I mean mainly their basic, essential, emotional needs.

The word "flourish" means to bloom, blossom, and do well. When children's needs are met, they are better able to have a solid foundation of value and self-worth. This will help them to have a strong identity, a sound sense of who they are, and the ability to love themselves. They can then blossom and be the beautiful and brilliant creatures they are.

As I said earlier, when you understand what your child needs, you are better able to provide it for them.

Children let us know in various ways if their needs are/aren't being met. This usually means they let us know through their behavior. Children's behaviors are usually about three needs-related questions:

1. Can you hear me? If not, then I will get louder or become voiceless.
2. Can you see me? If not, then I will try harder or become invisible.
3. Can I trust you to have my needs met? If not, then I will take risks in order to fulfill my own needs, or I will minimize, dismiss, and ignore my needs.

What Do Children Need?

1. Safety

Our very being depends on safety—physical and emotional safety, safe touch, and the belief that our world is generally a safe place. In order to help children make safe decisions, we need to make sure that their basic needs, especially safety, are fulfilled. People do not do well when they do not feel safe.

We tend to focus on physical safety, but emotional safety is just as important. Yes, it's important to have a safe space to hide, if necessary, but it's also important to have safe and brave spaces to be heard, to debrief, and to experience the emotional presence of a trusted other.

The need for safety must be in place in order for children to make good decisions, and it is important for you to understand that when children engage in risky behaviors, it can be a sign that they feel unsafe. As odd as it sounds, feeling unsafe can draw us to unsafe and dangerous activities.

I remember one day my middle child came home very upset and was giving me and her mom attitude. I asked if she was behaving the same way in school, and she replied, "Of course not," so I asked why then was she doing this at home. She answered, "Maybe because I feel safe at home." That statement stunned me. I thought, "Here we go, another shrink in the family." That statement was an eye-opener, children act out when they don't feel safe. Their behavior is just the message that something is wrong, and it is only when they have a safe caregiver that they feel they can have permission to unload that burden in order to lessen their anxiety and feel safe again. So as parents, we should make it easier for them by being available and willing to listen. If I had reacted differently that day by punishing her temper tantrum, I would have likely made things worse for all of us.

Making safety a priority means having zero tolerance for violence in any form or shape.

When it comes to safety within families, parents might show their love and affection differently to their children, which can be confusing or confirming. When we show love safely, our children won't feel they need to walk on eggshells around us.

Safe Touch. Safe touch is an essential need and a comfort for everyone, especially survivors of trauma.

Touch can feel awkward when it hasn't been yet established or after a period of time without it. For example, when I left my children for six months to help in disaster relief, they were very anxious and didn't know how to re-connect. It took us time to re-establish that bond. We arm wrestled, thumb-warred, and gave bear hugs. We played together, and they rode on my back, among many other things. I was willing to do whatever it took to bond again with my daughters.

Small gestures aren't small in the grand scheme of things. Sitting close while you read a book, snuggling, and telling bedtime stories. The last thing before bed is safety. Tuck them in. Kiss them. Say I love you. In some cultures, these small activities may be disparaged or discouraged. They are not silly; they are as important for your child's psyche and emotional wellbeing as explicitly telling them how important they are.

What about unsafe touch? What does a parent do when the child has been traumatized?

Unsafe touch, such as sexual assault, rape, or torture, can do severe damage because the child's body was touched, their voice was not valued, and boundaries were violated.

One of the foundations that is easily shattered after traumatic experiences of a physical or sexual nature is intimacy and the belief that you can love and be loved again.

Safe touch is one way we can bring intimacy back. Once a parent shows their children that they are uncon-ditionally loved regardless of how the children view them-selves, they will start to love themselves again and feel comfortable with touch.

This may take a significant amount of time, so par-ents need to practice lots of patience and self-restraint. Intimacy means "into me see," so pay close attention to your children's spoken and unspoken language.

This is the message that safe touch can create in a family:

- The space between us is always safe.
- You are safe around me, and I am safe around you.
- I will accept all of your actions and behaviors as long as they are safe. By saying you accept a behavior doesn't mean that you always agree with it.

Safe touch has healing powers, and it is worth the effort to meet this essential need.

Belief that the world is generally safe—and when it's not, our smaller world will be. How can we help our children believe the world is a safe place when bombs drop, armies invade, and predators attack? We cannot control the world, and we cannot stop bombs, shootings, and natural disasters. What we can create is a safe smaller world—our homes, extended families, and communities—where we do all we can to keep each other safe.

The smallest and largest of worlds is relationship, and **as parents it is our job to make our relationship with our children a place of absolute safety**. We are there to be sure our children are not abused or taken advantage of. One way to do that is to be authentic and model expressing your own feelings safely and calmly.

2. Attachment

What is attachment?

Attachment is how a child and parent or caregiver bond.

Think of it like this: If you are about to fall off a cliff, would you want to be attached to a very large rock or a small stone? Who is your child's rock? You, of course.

That is how attachment works for children. When they feel attached to an emotionally strong parent or caregiver, they feel safer. No matter what happens, they feel attached to a strong someone who will genuinely try to take care of them.

A child who doesn't feel attached will feel unsafe and on their own. They will search for someone else to bond to, often anyone who gives them attention. This can send them from one person to the next in a desperate search for someone to be their strong anchor, jeopardizing their safety in the process.

Attachment also makes it possible for children to withstand bullies and predators because they feel secure in their bond with their parents or caregivers. Attachment becomes their shielding armor.

How to improve your attachment with your child

1. Create a safe space for both spirit and body.
2. Make eye contact.
3. Be a warm presence and offer comfort.
4. Accept and validate your child's feelings.
5. Spend time together, one-on-one, without excessive technology or distractions.
6. Talk together with an open-door policy.
7. Speak well of your child.
8. Protect from outside harm as best you can.
9. Discipline without violence, shame, or unforgiveness.
10. Learn the art of smiling.

There are four major types of attachment styles:

- Secure—often displayed by children who have structure in their daily lives and are unconditionally loved. They feel somewhat anxious when their parent is absent but are quickly comforted when the parent returns.
- Avoidant—often displayed by abused children. They don't easily make eye contact and often feel safer when the parent is away. That sounds very sad, doesn't it?
- Ambivalent—often displayed by children who are neglected. Whether the parent is there or not it doesn't really matter much because their absence or presence is equally insignificant.
- Disorganized—often displayed by children getting mixed messages from the parent or caregiver. The parent goes back and forth between acting loving and abusive, confusing the children with the uncertainty of what is coming next: will they be cared for or intimidated.

These four attachment styles are also the four parenting styles. Secure children are a result of parents with a secure parenting style. We often adopt the parenting style of our parents because it is all that we have known. The good news is that you can improve your parenting style starting now. Begin by saying you want to raise secure children and then commit by making one small positive change at a time.

Traumatic events can impact the nature and quality of attachment.

What would cause a parent to shy away from attaching to their child, especially after trauma?

1. They hadn't formed an open door policy and comfort with their children back when things were "normal." I often see this with teenagers. They want to talk to us, but we don't know how to talk to them and they are left to nurse their own wounds. Many cry themselves to sleep, unnoticed. This is unfair to children today and can haunt you as a parent tomorrow. When you come later to talk to your teenage child you might be told that you have arrived too late. Scary, isn't it?

2. They are afraid they will cause more damage if they don't do it "right."

3. They may not have attached as children, and the idea sounds foreign and terrifying to them.

4. They are so focused on other things, they don't notice their child is not attaching.

Children deserve to have their need for attachment met. Parents need to learn how to attach so their children and families can easily bond. Be around your loved ones in a relaxed way. If your child shuts down when you walk into the house and relaxes when you exit, then you need to urgently and immediately change your ways.

Be encouraged to know that attachment can happen even later in life when a person is helped to make meaningful sense of their trauma story. It is never too late to change. When it comes to our loved ones, loving them is always the right thing to do.

3. Structure

Children need consistency through routine and structure, as they do not do well in chaos and uncertainty. However, flexibility is also important. Parents need to offer as many healthy, safe options and alternatives as possible.

Trauma increases the need for structure because some sense of sanity, normalcy, and routine is needed when there is chaos and when safety is not guaranteed.

4. Play

Children play. This is a good thing for many reasons, even at times of trauma. In situations and cultures where play is discouraged, children still find ways to do it. Play is a safe and powerful way for children to express their unspoken feelings and imagine and practice new situations and relationships.

Sometimes adults discourage children from playing because life is hard and even dangerous. It is important for us to understand that children must play. It is their way of coping and finding relief from the stress of life, especially when emergencies and crises are a part of that life—or have been.

For many traumatized children, play is their voice when they have no words to describe what happened to them.

Many parents don't have the energy to join in their children's activities, but play is a vital bonding affair at times of uncertainty and distress. If you can't join in, I urge you to at least openly appreciate and encourage their play. **Take care of yourself so you become available for them when they need you.**

Play and Trauma. Trauma disrupts the sense of security that a normally safe and harmless activity like play provides.

Children of trauma often use play as a way of speaking when they don't know how to share what has happened. Play becomes their voice.

Often children will re-enact the themes of their abuser(s), such as children of war who use their imagination to create games full of killing and violence. They relive their trauma through play.

Since children naturally use play as a language, play therapy can be a very helpful way for professionals to guide children to work through their trauma. Children are able to write or rewrite their own story, so to speak, regain their voice, and reclaim their narrative.

Parents can help by noticing changes that happen to their children, emotionally, behaviorally, academically, or socially. If in doubt, whenever there is a sudden change, believe in your gut feelings and follow your heart, gently enquire about the root causes of such change, and even if they don't share what is bothering them, offer your presence and let them know that your door is always open and that you will listen when they are ready to talk. Enlist available professional help if needed.

Play therapy is a powerful healing tool. It gives children a way to safely express their story and unspoken feelings. The rules of safe play therapy are the same rules of a safe family: stick together, have fun, and no one gets hurt.

Violence shatters the core ability to self soothe, regulate, and connect with others. Play helps restore that.

Play gives a child the chance to be heard, seen, and to feel trust again. You may recall that these are the three questions children constantly ask with their behavior to reassure themselves that they are safe and that their needs are being met.

How Children Develop

Children develop at their own pace, yet there are general steps to growth that most children follow. It is important for children to complete one phase before moving on to the next, so pushing them is not helpful.

This chart shows the themes of our development. Every time we don't progress through a theme, we risk having a conflict or even a psychological crisis. Healing from it can happen even at a later stage, but the earlier the better.

I suggest you become familiar with these developmental themes so you will be better able to know if your child doesn't move through them. It is like learning to read street signs. It will help you be a better guide for them when the world is unsafe.

Themes of human development by ages.
Dr. Erik Erikson

Birth to 18 mos:	*Trust vs. Mistrust*: Assure me that my world is safe and you can be trusted.
18 mos– 3 yrs:	*Autonomy vs. Doubt*: Assure me that my attempts at control please you. Give me encouragement and praise for my effort.
3–5 yrs:	*Initiative vs. Guilt and Shame*: Acknowledge and validate my plans and activities.
6–12 yrs:	*Industry vs. Inferiority*: I need to feel I can "make it" in the world and achieve.
13–19 yrs:	*Identity vs. Role Confusion*: I need to feel comfortable with who I am and achieve identity in occupation, gender roles, politics, and in some cultures, religion.
20–39 yrs:	*Intimacy vs. Isolation*: I want a validating love and meaningful relationships.
40–64 yrs:	*Generativity vs. Self-Absorption or Stagnation*: I need to feel productive and accomplished and to feel appreciated for what I do.
65 years and older:	*Integrity vs. Psychological Despair*: I reflect on what I have done for humanity and need to feel a sense of self-satisfaction about the legacy I am leaving behind.

The Rights of Children

Children have rights that are considered universal and sacred, as written by the Convention on the Rights of the Child, a part of the United Nations. I have summarized them for you here so you can be a strong advocate for your children and do what you can to protect their rights.

THE CONVENTION ON THE RIGHTS OF THE CHILD

No child should be treated unfairly on any basis, regardless of their race, religion, abilities, whatever they think or say, wahtever type of family they come from, where they live, what language they speark, what their parents do, whether they are boys or girls, what their culture is, whether they have a disability or whether they are rich or poor. (Article 2, Non-Discrimination)

The best interests of children must be the primary concern in making decisions that may affect them. All adults should do what is best for children. When adults make decisions, they should think about how their decisions will affect children. This particularly applies to budget, policy and law makers. (Article 3, Best interests of the child)

Children have the right to live. Governments should ensure that children survive and develop healthily. (Article 6: Right to life, survival and development)

When adults are making decisions that affect children, children have the right to say what they think should happen and have their opinions taken into account. This does not mean that children can now tell their parents what to do. This Convention encourages adults to listen to the opinions of children and involve them in decision-making -- not give children authority over adults. Article 12 does not interfere with parents' right and responsibility to express their views on matters affecting their children. Moreover, the Convention recognizes that the level of a child's participation in decisions must be appropriate to the child's level of maturity. Children's ability to form and express their opinions develops with age and most adults will naturally give the views of teenagers greater weight than those of a preschooler, whether in family, legal or administrative decisions. (Article 12: Respect for the views of the child)

https://www.unicef.org/crc/files/Guiding_Principles.pdf

"Children do not seek or crave attention, they deserve it, and it is their basic human right."

Dr. Omar Reda

Children and the Results of Trauma

Trauma doesn't just make it harder to be a child—it makes it harder to be an adult if there isn't healing from the trauma. In fact, depending on how children react to their trauma and the level of help they receive, they can grow up to repeat it or be unable to enjoy their lives because of painful memories that don't go away.

Trauma can change how children see themselves, the world, and what is possible for them. This can cause changes in behavior that make a child seem to be what they weren't before.

The good news is that children are resilient and can recover with the unconditional support of their caregivers.

A traumatized family is a special family, and if empowered, can be more and offer more. Trauma can make rather than break a family. A family that tackles trauma together and works as a team is strongly bonded, more welcoming, and more resilient.

I commend you for doing all you can to pry the fingers of trauma away from your child's life and future. If not untangled from their trauma, it can continue to affect them for life in various ways.

Post-Traumatic Stress Disorder (PTSD). PTSD is common after a traumatic event. Survivors may re-experience the traumatic intrusive memories through flashbacks and nightmares. Some try to avoid any reminders it ever happened. Others experience physical symptoms like shortness of breath, sweating, hand tremors, and heart palpitations when triggered.

It is as if the body is reliving the trauma again and again and the hormones meant to be used once in awhile for short-term survival are used repeatedly, harming the body in the long run.

In the case of children, PTSD can make them startle easily, become more clingy, regress and start acting younger than their chronological age. It can cause stomach pains and headaches, or show up as struggles in behavior, relationships, academic performance, and in school and home dynamics.

Forced Displacement. Forced migration or displacement to another country as a refugee can be traumatic for children. It is also the beginning of a new chapter of their lives, a chapter that can become an important and even heroic part of their story.

It is important to realize that refugees are normal people. They will be anywhere on a spectrum, so we need to be careful not to generalize. Not everyone is a victim and not everyone is a hero. We need to humanize them and listen with interest to their stories and celebrate their courage and resilience.

Children displaced to countries other than the one they were born in are sometimes called TCKs, or "Third Culture Kids." They are in the difficult position of wanting to honor the culture of their parents yet needing to adopt the culture of the country where they now live. To do this, they build their own "third culture" identity by combining aspects of both their homeland culture and that of their new home.

Third Culture Kids can feel like they don't belong anywhere. Here is what one young woman said about having people ask her the question, "Where are you from?"

> As a child I would scream when people uttered those four words. It sounds melodramatic, but at least my seven-year-old self was honest about the frustration I felt. A mix of confusion, anxiety, and sometimes even pain consumed

me. It's not socially acceptable to scream anymore when people ask that question. But that doesn't ease the difficulty. Most people think the pain is fake and pretentious or just a call for attention. Who cares if you're just a little bit more cosmopolitan and diverse than most people—deal with it. If anything, I am one of the lucky ones, right? Being exposed to a rich variety of cultures, histories, and traditions from a young age is only a privilege.

Perhaps it is, but with this privilege comes a significant degree of toxicity.

(Excerpt from https://raseef22.com/en/culture/2017/12/09/arab-third-culture-kids-tell-us-world/)

It can be very difficult for parents to watch their children weave a culture of their own from their homeland and their new country.

Parents naturally want to deepen their child's love of their cultural heritage, traditions, and values, including religious beliefs. When a child must adapt to a new country and culture, parents can feel hurt, frustrated, betrayed, alienated, and rejected. They often fear they will be tossed aside, too, and that their children will be further traumatized by a new culture that does not understand them.

Identity confusion is real and needs to be dealt with through education and compassion in order to prevent an identity crisis that carries heavy consequences. What is important is that parents and children work as a team through understanding this: **to have more than one culture should be seen as an advantage rather than a handicap, families should unite through this rather than see each other as the enemy.**

The message that is consistent throughout is, "We will get through this, together."

How Children Act Out Their Trauma

Traumatic events are many. Exposure to violence, especially of an intimate nature, can interrupt a child's development, and without intervention, it can change the course of a child's life and behavior.

Self-Harm

Cutting, burning, head-banging, starving, binge eating, purging, self-inflicted injuries, and suicide attempts are all examples of an attempt to reach out for help.

It is a sign that a child is feeling desperately hopeless and alone and that they are in urgent need of protection, soothing, and nurture.

Violence

It is said that hurt people can in turn hurt people. When children become violent, it is a sign of how out of control they feel. "Acting out" is only the message. Violence can be physical, sexual, verbal, emotional, or the threat of using lethal means. Rather than labeling the child as difficult, rebellious, or defiant, we need to look closely at the root causes and strive to fix them.

Impulsivity

Speeding, excessive spending, unsafe sexual practices, shoplifting, and fire-setting are some of the unhealthy coping skills that need correction, not punishment.

Dysfunctional Relations

Repeating the cycle of abuse is a theme that some trauma survivors can encounter.

Trauma is a family affair. Trauma is like cancer. Untreated, it quickly spreads throughout the body leading to severe, malignant, and even fatal consequences.

Anxiety

Bedwetting, hoarding, nail biting, skin picking, hair pulling, and obsessive-compulsive rituals are forms of anxiety. They can be attempts to self-soothe or regulate emotions, and can respond to psychotherapeutic interventions.

Substance Use

One of the most common ways to cope with trauma is to self-medicate either by using alcohol or another substance.

Facing traumatic memories and accompanied strong emotions is quite an unpleasant experience that many want to numb using drugs.

Post-traumatic stress disorder and substance use and abuse tend to commonly coexist.

Grief

There is no right or wrong way when it comes to mourning the loss of a loved one or even the loss of life as it used to be. Children's reactions to death and/or loss and their response to its aftermath are to be honored and respected as long as they are safe and healthy.

Anger

Some argue that anger is depression expressed externally (voiced-out), while others argue that depression is anger repressed internally (voiced-in). There is truth to both statements.

While we cannot necessarily choose our parents or change our genes, we can modify our current environment and regulate our emotions. Trauma complicates all of that, and hence it is important to acknowledge and address the trauma story, the big invisible elephant in many of our rooms.

Steps to Resolve Acting Out

Author and psychiatrist Bruce Perry suggests people cannot reason unless they can first relate, and that cannot happen unless they first regulate. Regulating means managing ourselves.

The steps to helping our children regulate, or manage, their emotions are:

1. Soothe the affect. In other words, calm their emotions, give comfort, and satisfy your child's need to be seen and heard.

2. Establish a connection. Remain available even if your child is angry or pushes you away. Be available without being intrusive. Say something like, "When you're ready, I'm here for you."

3. Work together on a reasonable solution to a conflict. Make your child a part of a solution you create together or with the help of others, including professionals.

4. We might not be equal in power, but we are equal in dignity, and we stick together and value one another as unconditionally lovable individuals and as a source of joy and delight.

Refer children to a specialist if they

- show prolonged symptoms of anxiety, sorrow, anger, or grief;
- lose academic or social progress;
- suffer from recurrent nightmares or night-terrors;
- hallucinate or have paranoid or obsessive thoughts;
- have changes in their core values, like engaging in deviant, dark ideologies;
- isolate or neglect themselves;
- use alcohol or other substances;
- have somatic symptoms like unremitting migraines, severe pains, and startle seizures;
- regress in age like bed-wetting, thumb-sucking, stuttering, or clinging;
- are suicidal or homicidal;
- have access to weapons or lethal means.

Adult Survivors of Childhood Trauma

Children who have survived trauma grow up to become adult children of trauma. Many of them also become parents. It is important for them to understand what trauma meant for them and how it has affected their

- Psyche
- Sense of self
- Confidence
- Ability to trust
- Relating and connecting to themselves and others
- Dependence on habits like drugs, self-harm, or repeating the maladaptive cycles

If you are a traumatized parent, here are few things to do to find relief and move toward healing:

1. Write a new story about your trauma, a story that helps you find meaning of your experience. Get help with this from your social and professional communities.

2. Create closure to your trauma by making amends and forgiving yourself.

3. End the cycle. Stop doing what keeps the trauma active in your parenting. The smallest improvement makes a big difference, and being open about your effort will help children know you care. Seek help and support to do this because changing behaviors that aren't good for us requires it, even if trauma has not been a part of our lives.

Words of Hope
(collected from different parenting sources):

- Persistence and consistency pay off, especially when combined with love and tender care.

- Most of us are quick to criticize but slow to praise. Our children's self-esteem is too valuable to be left to chance or entrusted to strangers. We need to fill their emotional buckets.

- The whole world will tell our children what is wrong with them, so let us tell them what is right with them and how joyful and honored we are to have them in our lives.

- When our children sense our delight in them, they breathe it in.

- Appreciation is shown through actions, and it is always welcome even if it comes late.

- The message that our children need to always hear is that **we love them unconditionally**.

Notes

What do you want to remember from this section?

What help do you need?

What next steps will you take to get that help?

What words of hope do you want to give to your child?

What words of hope do you want to give to yourself?

Other things you want to note:

PART 3: FAMILIES

WE ARE FAMILIES OVERCOMING TRAUMA
Resilient beings bonded by times of distress and delight,
We light our way,
Skilled in healing, unconditional and accepting.
Safe and at ease, Hope sees.

Part 3: Family

Now let's widen our focus from children to families.

What a Family Is

A family is a fascinating group of people connected to one another by birth or marriage. The members of a family are unique, opinionated, and gifted with talents and personalities that can both strengthen and challenge them. It is an amazing thing to see a family come together and, even better, stick together through whatever comes.

A family is

- the foundation of a healthy society;
- the glue that holds loved ones in times of distress and delight;
- a healing environment;
- a safe space when the world becomes dangerous or unpredictable;
- an umbrella of unconditional love and acceptance;
- where members feel safe and at ease;
- where we can be our true, authentic selves.

A traumatized family can be all of this and more.

A traumatized family, if empowered, can be more and offer more:

- bonded in times of distress and delight;
- skilled in healing;
- resilient when the world becomes dangerous or unpredictable;
- unconditional and accepting;
- safe and at ease;
- welcoming of each other's true selves.

Families and Trauma

As in a terrorist attack, trauma can strike a peaceful family unit suddenly, leading to an assault on its very moral foundation.

If family members decide to deny, ignore, or blame one another for the changes the trauma brings to their family dynamics, they risk losing their cohesive system and identity to the trauma.

But if, on the other hand, they actively invest in compassion and communication, then bridges of resilience get built to lead them on their journey toward closure and healing.

A family that actively tackles trauma together is a very special family that ends up with a strong backbone and a mosaic of harmony.

What Helps and What Doesn't

Trauma impacts the entire family, including the extended family. How your family copes and recovers can depend on the nature of the trauma itself, the age of your children, your culture, and your unique style of coping. It can also depend on how well you are able to maintain your family functions and get the help you need.

What Helps:

Safe and nurturing relationships between parents, children, and the extended family will help you recover and grow after trauma.

Have some fun. Fun can be healing, and it is said that laughter is like medicine. Families that play together stay together. Families living with trauma need the medicine of fun together.

- Go on a hike.
- Watch positive movies and empowering shows.
- Make a video of yourselves doing something fun.
- Make art, or go to a place where art is created.
- Build things together.
- Play games.
- Take photos on a walk.
- Take up a sport.
- Tell a joke.

The National Child Traumatic Stress Network suggests the following factors can make it more difficult, but not impossible, for families to regain a sense of safety and stability:

- psychiatric history in the family,
- increasing life stressors,
- prior traumas or adverse childhood experiences (ACEs),
- conflict or violent family interactions,
- social isolation,
- limited resources.

The good news is that a traumatized family can use their history, trauma story, and vulnerability to collectively grieve, heal, and build long-lasting resilience. It is said that **vulnerability is the ultimate act of courage**. Be courageous.

It is easier said than done, but not impossible. I often see it happen right before my eyes.

What doesn't help is the opposite—families that blame and alienate one another, families that avoid or deny the trauma or take each other for granted, and families that knowingly or unconsciously repeat the cycle.

The Trauma of Family Forced Displacement

Families face many types of trauma in today's world. I am going to focus on one that is more common these days: forced relocation. By focusing on this, I am not minimizing the importance or difficulties of other traumas.

Earlier in the book I spoke about the topic of TCKs— Third Culture Kids. I'd like to look at it again from the perspective of a family.

Families experience huge stress when displaced, relocated, or forcibly migrated to another country. The parents identify with the country they come from, and their children identify more quickly with the new country.

This has a profound effect on the family dynamics and can cause conflict between generations.

Acculturation means adapting to a new culture without the pressure to fully assimilate and lose one's identity in the process.

Here are two examples from TheDimensionsOfCulture.com:

1. A father loses his traditional role as head of the family when his wife begins to work outside the home. She earns money and greater independence. This disrupts how the parents relate to each other. At the same time, his children adopt the attitudes and values of the new culture, making him feel like he is losing touch with his children. He loses confidence in his role, feels undignified, and can withdraw or grow angry.

2. The children of a displaced family learn the language of the new country and become interpreters for their parents and grandparents. This puts the children in touch with information normally not suited for them, such as legal, financial, and health issues. The parents must look to the children for help, which could upset the parent-child dynamic.

What situations have you experienced or observed like this?

The conflict between cultures puts unnecessary distance between members of the family at a time when **being together in loving ways is what is needed for healing**.

Families are an ever-changing mix as people are added, others pass, and times change. Culture plays a big role in how families develop, so we will focus there.

All families are part of a particular culture or mix of different cultures. Our cultures hold deep-rooted ideas about how we should feel, think, and act, and what we should believe. Parents are expected to pass this along to their children.

Cultures take very different approaches to parenting:

Western/European Cultures	Collective Cultures (American Indian, Asian, Hispanic, African, Middle Eastern)
Value individuality, uniqueness, self-reliance, and private life	Absolute loyalty to family over self
Train children to think and make decisions for themselves	Decisions are made by family, extended family, and sometimes elders
Generations live separately	Generations live together
Decisions are personal	Decisions are usually collective, made with the whole family's best interest in mind

Place a check on the column your family most identifies with.

Culture and Trauma

The strong ideas cultures carry about parenting can affect how families in those cultures manage trauma.

Both cultures are very proud and have difficulty asking for help.

The independent nature of western cultures causes families to take trauma on by themselves. They do everything they can on their own before asking for help in order to remain in charge of their own choices and outcomes. They have an attitude of "I can do this."

The interdependent nature of collective cultures causes families to keep the trauma under wraps because of loyalty to the family and its secrets. They have an attitude of "I can't burden others."

The nature of trauma is to ruin what it touches, so keeping your family from receiving the help and compassion it needs to heal may not be in anybody's best interest.

Helping your family heal from trauma is a noble priority, and I encourage you to work with, or through, your cultural baggage to do that, if necessary.

How is your culture influencing the way you are managing your family's trauma?

Are you happy with the results?

If not, how can you use your culture or religion as a healing, rather than a hindering, tool?

How can parents and caregivers ease the trauma of forced displacement? (Most of this advice is true for other kinds of trauma; we just need to respect the cultural context.)

Here are some ways TCKs parents can support their children:

- Put yourself in their shoes.

  Trauma has terrorized you and forced you to leave the life you knew before. Perhaps you have had to leave loved ones behind, and you are worried for their safety. In the meantime, you must learn a new language and way of life in order to make it in your new country. You feel panicked that you won't know how to fit in. You hide your feelings and fears from your family because you feel they have been through enough. You work hard to be "strong," but inside you are afraid, terrified, confused and at the same time curious about your new world.

- Be real about the situation.

  Pretending everything is OK when it isn't doesn't help things get better. I don't mean you need to hash over awful details or stories that bring you down. I do mean you can be real about the basic facts of what your family has experienced and what is happening now. This keeps your children from believing you want them to hide what's real for them. Healthy expression, processing, acceptance, and sorting of emotions is encouraged in a safe house.

- Reassure them you are there for them, and prove it.

  Children know you cannot meet every need they have in this new country every single time, but they do need to trust you will be there **with them** through it all. You can be a team that works together to figure things out and get the help you need.

  It is the <u>being with</u> that matters.

- Share your own feelings.

  Even if you have not been a family that shares feelings, you can begin now. A simple statement like, "I know we haven't been a family who shares our feelings easily, things are different now. It's important for us to be there for one another, and sharing feelings is one way we can do that." Then prove you mean it by being more open about your feelings in a respectful way. Over time, your children may follow your example, and even if they don't, your openness will be helpful to them. An open parent is usually a safe parent.

- Find people, groups, and resources to help.

  Your job is to get your children what they need to thrive. You are your children's chief advocate. You are their voice and loyal support. You watch out for them and keep an eye out and ears open to people and groups who can help your children heal and succeed in their new world.

- Educate yourself on the laws and parenting culture of your new country.

  Knowing the rules and ways of a country can prevent the kind of cultural misunderstandings that can put your right to parent in question and your children at risk. Find out and be familiar with the laws in your new country about children, parenting, and families.

- Remain kind, consistent, respectful, and loving.

  Love heals, as does kindness and respect. Do for your children what you would want done for you if you were in their position, and a little more. When it comes to your family there is no such thing as too much love. When it comes to your family, you can't afford anything less than your best, because they deserve it, and you do too. Your family is worth it.

- Choose what you want to be true of you.

  Who you are and what you do is up to you. What do you want to be true of you, and what words will you want to hear from your children when they talk about this period of time in your family's life?

Here are some examples to get you thinking:

☐ "My mother/father were with me when I needed safety and comfort."

☐ "Even when things were at their worst, we stayed strong together."

☐ "I remember my father calling us together and saying that it was important for all of us to share our feelings, and we did, even though we hadn't really done that before."

☐ "I know it broke my parents' hearts to see me adopt the ways of my new world, but they understood."

☐ "My parents did a good job finding help for us and things to do to help us heal and get through the hard times."

Place a check mark by the statements you want to be true of you.

Here is some space for you to write what you would hope your children would say of you in years to come:

I can't guarantee they will use those exact words, but you will know in your heart that you lived in a way that deserves them.

What Families Need

Here is my list of the top five things a family needs other than safety and the physical basics of food, water, and shelter:

1. love;
2. togetherness;
3. open, respectful communication;
4. attention, affection, and appreciation;
5. hope.

What else would you add to this list? Invite your family to add to it. Check the item(s) you and your family believe you do best. Circle the item(s) you and your family most want to improve. I suggest you write those on a piece of paper and post it somewhere in your home as a reminder. Then take action.

What Traumatized Families Need

Traumatized families have the same needs as all families, plus these.

1. Access to extra help, such as extended family, neighbors, friends, and community and professional resources.
2. Information to help manage their unique situation.
3. Loyalty through times that can pull others apart.
4. Patience to allow healing.
5. Positive attitude.
6. Hope.

What would you and your family add to this list?

What is your family's most important need right now? Be very specific.

Knowledge means half the battle is won. You can sit down and work on solutions together.

Starting with What Is

Sometimes simply saying what has happened and acknowledging it together can get the healing started, even though other therapeutic interventions may be necessary.

What is true of you and your family right now? Here is a list of what is true for many traumatized families. Check the ones that are true for you:

- ☐ We have been traumatized.
- ☐ My children and I don't talk much.
- ☐ I don't know what to do.
- ☐ I feel guilty.
- ☐ I want to be a good parent but don't know how.
- ☐ I find myself making things worse.
- ☐ I am an overprotective helicopter parent.
- ☐ I am preoccupied with the trauma that has happened.
- ☐ I prefer to focus on visible wounds, not invisible ones.
- ☐ I chase after solutions to my physical needs more than my emotional ones.
- ☐ In our home, the F-word we avoid is Feelings.
- ☐ I notice people walking on eggshells around me.
- ☐ I feel hopeless and afraid most of the time.
- ☐ My children seem to feel badly about themselves.
- ☐ I seem uncomfortable around my loved ones.
- ☐ I tend to either isolate or lash out, and the easy target for my outbursts is my family.

What else would you add?

What else is true of your family?

Each of the situations on this list can be improved, and often when one thing improves, other things do, too.

When we parents set a good example of self-care and healing, our children often sense the change and welcome the new energy.

Healing our Troubled World, one smile at a time

Your Family's Style

Your family has a unique style, and like culture, it will help or hinder healing from trauma.

These are four examples of family styles:

- Authoritative: Parents are attentive, set guidelines, support their children's interests, and encourage open communication.

  Trauma is a family affair, and healing from trauma is a parent-led, family effort, and they are all in it together.

- Authoritarian: Parents are strict, quick to punish, and demand obedience rather than encourage communication.

  Trauma is often dismissed and "healing" from trauma may be forced or hurried.

- Neglectful: Parents are often absent or unaware of their children's needs.

  Healing from trauma will not happen without an outside help or a "wakeup call."

- Permissive: Parents are not consistent, avoid setting rules and guidelines, and don't like to confront their children's negative behaviors.

  Healing from trauma will be a confusing on and off according to the general mood of the household.

What family style is closest to yours?

What might you adjust so that healing is more likely?

This Is Us, Together

The truth is, trauma has entered your family. There is no getting around it, but there are ways through it. You and your family have more to untangle than families who have not been terrorized by trauma, and you may feel, at times, like healing is impossible or out of reach.

One of the most helpful steps to healing can begin right now, with you.

I call it your *This Is Us, Together* declaration. Together, you can declare what is true now, and together, you can declare what you want your future to be.

Here is an example of a This Is Us, Together declaration that could be true of many of the families I work with:

- ☐ We are a family who stands together, like a team.
- ☐ We have experienced trauma.
- ☐ We are more resilient because of our trauma story.
- ☐ We will not let the past ruin our future.
- ☐ We were together through the trauma, and we will stay together through future struggles.
- ☐ We respect one another's rights to heal in our own ways.
- ☐ We do not let each other struggle alone.
- ☐ We will not hide our pain to protect each other.
- ☐ We will do what we need to do to bring healing.
- ☐ We will be there for each other because we are worth it.
- ☐ We are strong, smart, brave, kind, and determined.

- ☐ We listen and learn from each other.
- ☐ We use our trauma as proof of our strength and not as an excuse for negative behavior.
- ☐ We make our home a safe and caring place.
- ☐ We are each other's shield and have zero tolerance for any form of violence.
- ☐ We tackle issues as a team.
- ☐ We use every single resource available to us.
- ☐ We believe loving one another is our greatest healing power.

Place a check mark by the statement(s) your family wants to make true.

Add other statements here:

How do families go about creating their This Is Us, Together declaration?

Families are different in their degree of comfort about things like this. For a family that is securely attached, a family meeting is comfortable. For families that are more distant, there are more gentle approaches to being with your child without being suffocating or coming across as fake. It is being physically and emotionally available that matters.

If you're a hands-on family, jump in and create your declaration.

Find a simple way to introduce the activity to your family, something that works for you and is comfortable for the family. Don't overthink it, though. Be sincere, and trust your intention.

Rumi eloquently directed our attention to the importance of human connection as the foundation of relationships. He shared the deep reflection that many would look at either the value of the number one or the number two in the simple equation of (one and one make two), but very few would appreciate the value of (and). It is the spirit of a family that says, "This is us, and we are greater together."

Togetherness is the foundation of the entire Untangled work. Together, we can heal and flourish.

Words of Hope

- Tiny and "fragile" children don't deserve anything but love.
- Traumatized families are not "damaged goods."
- Trauma can make rather than break a family.

Notes

What do you want to remember from this section?

What help do you need?

What next steps will you take to get that help?

Notes

What do you want to remember from this section?

What help do you need?

What next steps will you take to get that help?

What words of hope do you want to give to your child?

What words of hope do you want to give to yourself?

Other things you want to note:

PART 4: PARENTS

WE ARE PARENTS OUTSMARTING TRAUMA,
Unstoppable guardians of our children's future well-being,
Freeing the tangled,
Igniting courage to take on the world.
Trauma steals, Hope heals.

Part 4: Parents

Now let's turn our focus to parents and caregivers.

What a Parent Is

Parents and caregivers are people who willingly take on the care of the world's most precious treasures—children. It is not an easy choice; in fact, it is full of headache, heartache, but also great joy.

Parents are children who have grown up to become parents themselves. They have their own sets of needs, fears, dreams, and stories that they often set aside for—or away from—their children.

As parents, caregivers, and community leaders, we can use the power of our human connections to build healing bridges of trust and open channels of communication with our children in ways that can prevent or reduce the effects of trauma and steer young generations toward a more positive and empowering future.

As parents, we can make or break our children.

- Build them up or tear them down.
- Empower or discourage them.
- Reassure or shut them down.
- Inspire or depress them.
- Welcome or reject them.

No amount of abuse experienced by the parent or care-giver should "excuse" a caregiver betraying that trust children place in them—what happened to you explains but never excuses what you do to others.

Our children take on what we are, so what we are matters.

A parent is the

- igniting source of courage when a child is ready to take on the world;
- the guiding source of light when the world gets darker;
- the warm source of comfort when the world becomes overwhelming or unsafe;
- the protective armor that is tough on the exterior and pleasantly gentle on the interior.

A parent of a traumatized child is someone who is

- caring for a child who was subjected to trauma;
- carrying the extra weight of tending to their child's new physical and emotional needs;
- trying to make sense of a chaotic world, for themselves and for their children;
- capable of reducing, and even healing, the effects of trauma on their children.

What Parents Need

All people have certain needs that must be met. These include:

- ☐ Physical needs
- ☐ Intellectual stimulation
- ☐ Social contact
- ☐ Emotional connection
- ☐ Spiritual satisfaction

Parents needs include the following:

- ☐ Parental training
- ☐ Healing from their own troubles and trauma
- ☐ Support and input
- ☐ Inspiration and aspiration
- ☐ Healthy habits
- ☐ Interests and hobbies
- ☐ Optimism
- ☐ Forgiveness, especially self-forgiveness

Look over this list and mark the needs that seem to be satisfied right now in your life, at least to a degree you're OK with. Of those that you haven't marked, which one(s) will you improve as you develop yourself as a human and parent?

How Parents Develop

Parenting is one of the most challenging and rewarding experiences a human can have. It is also the most important role we can play in our children's lives.

It is rare for parents to develop themselves as vigorously as they do for their jobs. It's such an odd thing to think we'll be great parents without learning how. The prevailing idea is to do our best and call it good (or make excuses). We are afraid we are going to "screw up" and hurt our kids, and we say we want to do our best, yet our best is not always good enough.

Our children deserve more.

How badly do you want your children to flourish? Do you even believe they can, especially if trauma has visited them?

Questions like these help you develop as a parent. While it's helpful to learn to parent through experience, or by following or unfollowing the way your parents did it, or even mimicking the example of your friends and society, it is most helpful to learn what children need to flourish and adjust the way you parent to it.

Good parenting is a skill that can be developed like any other skill. You study, watch, practice, and seek special help to get it right.

Here are ten examples of ways to develop as an effective parent.

1. Get smart about what children need to flourish. Read books, listen to talks, watch videos, join online parenting communities.

2. Ask for input from people whose parenting you respect.

3. Decide who you want to be as a parent and keep working toward it. Turn your list into a screensaver or vision board.

4. Decide what you will value as a parent. Honesty? Fun? Openness? Togetherness? Learning? Self-expression? Adventure? Curiosity? Generosity? Community? Make a list and live by it.

5. Be curious. Ask friends what puzzles them about parenting. Ask older parents what they would do differently or the same. Ask your children what they'd like to be as a family. Wear a t-shirt: "Parent in Training." Who isn't?

6. Heal your own troubles and trauma. Seek qualified help.

7. Bring your talents and hobbies into your parenting. It will become part of your legacy.

8. Sleep, eat, and exercise so your body can support your dreams.

9. Reach out for help when you need it. No one can parent alone even if they seem like they can. It does take a village.

10. Commit to being your child's most brave, loving, and loyal asset.

Your greatest power as a parent is to unconditionally love your children into feeling good about themselves so they can blossom and flourish and pursue a life that is strong and good for them and others. If every child reached their full potential, the world would indeed be a much better place for all.

I am not suggesting your journey will be a smooth ride or a quick fix—no journey is, especially when trauma is a part of it. Think of it instead as an imperfect climb on a long, worthy, upward spiral where love for your children is your highest priority. A walk inside a long, dark tunnel, where with perseverance, you emerge a better version of yourself.

Everything you do will improve with your warm presence, open attitude, unconditional love, and willingness to acknowledge what is true in your family—with confidence that together you can improve it.

Parents and Trauma

Trauma can suck the joy out of parenting.

How do you see parenting? Your answer may change from day to day, or even moment to moment. In tough times, you may say it is dreadful, depleting, discouraging, disheartening, disappointing, and even depressing. You may see it as a daunting task and even feel defeated.

What do you think about the idea of parenting being delightful?

Is it possible when your child has been traumatized?

Yes, it is. It might seem far-fetched right now,

but with strong conviction, investment, and hard work, it is an achievable goal.

Here is how we can learn to nourish our children so they flourish and enjoy a healthy level of self-worth in spite of the trauma that took it away.

1. We show a consistent, warm presence to prove to our children that despite the world's dark side, and despite their own feelings of worthlessness, they can experience beauty, healing and joy.

   By "warm presence" I mean our children find us welcoming, supportive, and there for them, regardless. We are reliably in their corner, **thinking the best of them and giving our best to them.**

2. We recognize and receive our children's doubts about their own identity and self-worth and acknowledge that it is a common outcome of trauma, an injury that we will address and heal together.

3. We challenge and counteract their distorted thinking patterns that are telling them no one loves them and there's no hope for them. We do this by showing them we love them and that we believe in them, unconditionally.

   We do this with our words and our actions. They hear us say:

   - "I value my children above everything else,"
   - "I love coming home to be with my children,"
   - "I believe the sky's the limit for my wonderful children."

They watch us set aside other things to be with them. They see us rearrange a space in the house and in our busy schedules to help them study or pursue a hobby. They feel us hold them, sit close as we watch movies on the sofa together, and laugh, talk, or play together.

These kinds of words and actions gradually disprove the belief they hold that they aren't worthy, and open the door to self-acceptance, love, and healing.

4. What has worked for you? It is very possible that you, too, have struggled to think well of yourself. The very same discouraging words in your child's head may have occupied yours, or still do.

How do you counteract your own feelings of low worth? What has been helpful to you can be helpful to your children (or not), but the bond you create by sharing with them what has helped you might help all of you.

Please remember, I am not the expert when it comes to your family. You are. And each family is unique. This is not a step-by-step manual; it is a go-to guide with information, ideas, and techniques you can use to bring love, hope, and healing into your home. It is a flexible approach that takes the body, mind, and spirit into consideration; in other words, the whole picture that includes your culture and experience.

As a parent, you are the most important person in your child's life.
Let that fact sink in. Believe it, cherish it, embrace it, and act upon it.

Parental Absence

No one can give the child affection and sense of safety more than the child's own parents.

When the parent is absent, it leaves a deep void in the child's heart that no one else can fill and a wound in their psyche that no one else can heal.

When a child is threatened by parental absence they might

- take the role of the parent and carry unfair responsibilities on their shoulders, or hold themselves to unreasonable standards, which might lead to hostility or aggression in order to protect self and others;
- become extremely anxious, which could manifest as irritability or hyperactivity;
- become fearful and start to withdraw or isolate;
- become depressed or suicidal.

An absent parent is always welcome to return, even if they have been "missing in action" for years or decades. Healing can and should happen (better late than never). A neglected child might need time and space to reconnect. An absent parent should respect that and never lose hope. We cannot give up on our children. Neither can we force them. Rather, we must be patient.

The Marks of an Empowering Parent

Like me, you want to be a parent that empowers your children. Here is a short list we can use to guide us.

Empowering Parents

1. Meet their children on both sides of the spectrum. On one side the children need to explore the world, and if I am an anxious parent, I will limit their potential. On the other end of the spectrum, you nurse their wounds when they return from their adventures needing comfort. Fathers are almost non-existent in some cultures and therefore are often unavailable and are especially encouraged and invited to explore the world with their children—jump inside their world and play with them.

2. Give their children room to breathe and explore the world.

3. Welcome and nurture the children when the world is no longer a safe place.

4. Encourage the children to fulfill their own potential, rather than the parent's plans for them. Don't relive your childhood through them.

5. Get on the same team, even if separated or divorced, so there will be consistency and so that the child's sense of safety will remain relatively intact.

6. Support the interests of each child with attention, praise, and whatever resources are within reach. Each child is unique; love them uniquely.

7. Teach responsibility. A safe home has boundaries, rules, responsibilities, and chores. Children are to be held to realistic expectations and consequences. There needs to be some level of predictability. Children don't do well facing the unknown.

Disciplining Your Child

On this last point, slapping or spanking a child is a cruel act and is now seen by modern practitioners as an adult temper tantrum. It reinforces the myth that violence can be resolved through violence. The parent becomes the focus of the child's anger and resentment.

It is a widely accepted belief in the field of child development that physical punishment deprives children of a much-needed learning skill, namely facing the consequences of their own decisions.

It is normal for children to reach for control when they feel anxious, scared, or out of control, so caregivers need to give up the struggle for control and focus on building a foundation of trust and safety rather than shaking their child's sense of safety through cruel punishment.

It is neither punishment nor reward that really works but rather the genuine validation of our children's feelings and experiences, and the empathic stand toward their struggles and distress.

The authors of *Raising a Secure Child* suggest that children don't misbehave to get attention; they do it to hide their true need. They would rather suffer the consequences of their misbehavior than let us know what they really need, mostly because they want to protect us or themselves from the emotional discomfort. Isn't that heartbreaking?

There are alternatives to hurting your child to train them to behave.

- Safely ignore the action, unless it is dangerous.
- Spend a time-in together (time-outs are out).
- Distract the child.
- Talk it through.

I understand this may go against some cultures of parenting. **Loving guidance done smartly will create the safety your child needs to feel secure and attached.**

As shared by Jane Nelsen of Positive Discipline, the 5Rs of positive parenting are:

1. Be Respectful of the child (no naming, shaming, blaming, defaming, or pain).
2. The consequence must be Related to the behavior. (If I do not brush my teeth, I get no candy.)
3. There is a Reasonable duration for the consequence.
4. Consequences must be Revealed in advance and shared with the child.
5. Have the child Repeat the agreement back to you, to make sure they understand it.

These are simple techniques. They can be used easily, and while you may not see a change immediately, you will see change if you are consistent.

Realistic Expectations and Consequences

What do I mean by realistic?

- Appropriate for the developmental and emotional age.
- Respectful to a child's way of thinking and style of interaction.
- Every child is unique the way they are, and that is to be celebrated.
- If the child struggles to be responsible, we as parents should pause and reflect: are we asking too much of the child because of a skill deficit, or have we not armed the child with the needed and necessary tools? "Clean your room" is a paralyzing directive. Clean the room with them a few times to teach them how it is done.

What about Consequences?

- Always safe and respectful.
- Violence has no place in a safe home.
- Verbal violence is as bad as physical punishment.
- Related to the offense. Not something outrageous.
- When you are angry, never retaliate; watch your actions and words. Your child is not your punching bag.
- A deliberate parent is proactive, not reactive.
- Take mistakes as opportunities for the children to learn, rather than opportunities for us to take revenge or vent our own frustration.

- We can look at the struggle as our common enemy and tackle it as a team. Our children should never be seen as the enemy.

- Time out is out. It is an outdated and confusing practice. Rather, you are going to have time in where we will figure things out together. It is well worth the extra few minutes.

- If you don't put your books together, we will not go to the library. If you are misusing your time on the laptop, we won't watch your favorite movie this week. These are common examples of what we sometimes say to get our children to comply.

- But a better approach is the use of positive language: if you brush your teeth, clean your room, use technology appropriately, then . . . (best gifts are emotional rather than materialistic).

- Offer space to consider consequences.

- Cultural "crimes" that go against a family's belief system need to be sensitively tackled. Sit down together as a group, as a family, or small community circle. What is the issue? What are the facts? What caused it? Together, we brainstorm the solution. The offender is part of the solution. This is a commonly used practice in restorative justice: "admit fault, apologize, make amends, and get integrated." Children will continue to make mistakes. It is not the end of the world if they do.

- We know the other way is not working: getting angry and grounding or hurting them. They will find ways to rebel. **The last thing you want to lose is your child or their emotional connection to you.**

Your Children Love You

A young son scratched letters into his father's new car. The child and the father saw the act in two different ways. The father was furious that his son would damage his car like this. He lost control and struck his son's fingers with a stick to teach him a lesson. Later, as his rage subsided, the father let the words his son had written sink into his heart: "Dad, I love you."

Your children love you, even if they act otherwise. No matter what, your children love you. And they want you to love them back.

You Don't Have to Be Perfect (and your children don't have to be either)

Many parents aspire to be perfect. If you carry that dream, I invite you to give it up. Perfection is not possible, and the energy you spend trying to make things perfect takes away from the quality time and energy you can spend on enjoying the relationship.

For example, if I worry that the house is spotless all the time, it will make the relationship with my family miserable. Making messes is part of how children grow; they learn through play.

It does not take away from your parenthood to apologize, compromise, and even let your children make non-critical decisions. It adds to it and relieves everyone, including you, from having to be perfect. Your openness makes healing possible.

The reason I am saying you shouldn't work hard to be perfect is because you are perfect for your children the way you are. You can fine-tune things, but you can and should also relax.

You have the best interest of your children at heart, and you do the best you can, knowing you will make mistakes along the way. You accept and forgive yourself unconditionally in the same way you do for your children. Imagine the positive impact this will have on the healing and future of your family.

You will not be a perfect parent. No one can be. You can be a very present, open, smart, supportive, and positive parent most of the time. Remember that **connection, not perfection, is the goal**.

Taking Care of Yourself

You don't ask your car to run on an empty tank, but you ask it of yourself. Being a parent is consuming and exhausting, and being a parent of a traumatized child is even more so.

We can and will fall apart if we don't take care of ourselves. Our first reaction to this advice is often, "Where will I find the time?" Then we say, "I don't have the energy" when children need us to interact and join their play.

It is amazing how little time it takes to refresh ourselves. Our bodies and spirit thrive on small spurts of attention. What can you do to insert self-care into your day? Jumping jacks? Five deep breaths? Ten minutes of meditation? When I come home, I sit in the driveway for a couple of minutes to unwind, breathe, and center myself before I enter the house to be with my girls.

Take care of yourself so you can take care of your children and the results of their trauma.

When You Are Depleted

It is common to become depleted and even disgruntled as a parent. What can we do to be loving at those times? Here are some suggestions.

1. Let your kids recharge you. Mutual nourishment is an interesting idea that has always made sense to me. It's easy to think as parents that we are the only ones who should give emotional nourishment, but it can be mutual. Our children can nourish us if we let them. When I come home too tired to give any more, I walk through the door. My daughters jump on me, and my batteries are recharged; my tank is refilled. I am then able to reciprocate affection and fill their emotional buckets. This is a fine balance, though, and can make for a slippery slope. I never advise for the child to be the sole source of nurture and healing for their parents; rather, both are part of the healing movement.

2. Pause and take care of yourself. Close your eyes. Breathe deep. Drink some water. Take a five-minute walk in the fresh air. Listen to some comedy. Take a nap. Brain surgeons, air pilots, and train drivers take breaks, so why don't you? Your job is as delicate as theirs. You deal with a malleable and potentially-fragile psyche. **You mold and build a human. Take that very seriously.**

3. Leave your problems at work. Make a conscious decision to leave any work-related problem out of the house.

4. Wait to get online until after you spend quality time with your children, or preferably, after they go to bed.

How to Love When You Yourself Feel Unloved

Like many parents, you may be running on an empty tank. By that, I mean your own buckets of safety, love, and attention may not have been filled by your parents when you were young, in spite of their best efforts to care for you, given their circumstances.

It is possible that your emotional needs were unfulfilled, ignored, dismissed, neglected, or even abused.

So how can you break the cycle of trauma and give love to your children when you yourself feel unloved? Can you give what you didn't receive? Here are a few suggestions:

1. Talk to yourself with kindness. Positive self-dialogue lets us talk to ourselves with the love we needed to hear when we were children.

    a. "Nice work being patient with the children today."
    b. "I can do this."
    c. "I am getting better and better at being a positive parent."

2. Treat your body with tender, loving care. We parent better when we feel better, and the way to feel better is to treat our bodies with the love and respect they deserve. Plus, it teaches your children how to do it.

    a. Insert one more healthy food into your day.

    b. Move ten minutes in a way that feels good: stretch, walk, run.

    c. Sleep so you can recover and be ready to meet the next day refreshed.

3. Improve how you cope. Coping skills can be learned. There are classes available in the community and online. How you cope with life determines the quality of your life and how well you are able to love yourself and lead your family to healing from trauma.

    a. Smile three times more than you do now.

    b. Praise twice as much as you complain.

    c. Listen more.

    d. Reach out instead of lashing out when you feel frustrated.

Choose one habit to develop at a time. Go from easiest to more challenging. What if you talked nicer to yourself twice as often as you do now? What if you ate more fruits or drank a few more cups of water? What if you stopped yourself from reacting impulsively twice as often as you do now? Take small, steady steps.

These are acts of love for yourself, and they will begin to fill your own buckets of safety, love, and attention.

Our children don't deserve anything less than every single ounce of our healing love and tender care.

The Power of Words, Looks, and Gestures

You know the power of words because you have been lifted by them and wounded by them. So have your children.

At any given moment, we as parents choose whether to speak words that build our children up or tear them down. All of us have spoken words we wish we could take back, and it is important to apologize when we do.

However, apologies are empty when we routinely hurt our children with words. It is called verbal abuse. It can be every bit as traumatic as physical abuse.

It is said that "mean words are weapons that children store and can later use to hurt themselves or others." Also, "You will never feed or clothe your children with unhealthy or harmful stuff, so why talk to them in a toxic way?" Children should be viewed as part of the solution and not only as part of the problem.

In some ways, explosions inside the house are more harmful than outside. The words that a parent uses to crush a child's spirit can be more harmful than a bomb.

As a psychiatrist, a large portion of the abuse my clients experience is verbal. Many of them say they would have preferred a slap in the face than hear the words that were spoken to them.

Words. Here are some common examples of words that empower and words that defeat:

I'm so lucky to be your parent.

I wish I'd never had you.

I delight in you regardless of your achievements.

You'll never amount to anything.

You are never a burden to me.

Life would be easier without you.

You can express your feelings here.

Keep your feelings to yourself.

My door is always open to you.

I've got problems of my own; I don't need yours, too.

Crying is a good thing and courageous.

Crying is for sissies.

Have fun.

You're a goof off.

I love watching you find your talents.

You're the one in this family who can do nothing good.

You are strong.

Don't be so weak.

You don't need to bear this load like a grown-up.

You are the man of the house.

Girls are just as capable as boys.

Girls don't do that.

I hope you do what makes you happy.

I know better than you what will make you happy.

What words have helped you? Write them here:

I encourage you to include these positive words in your conversations with your children. Write them in notes to them to carry in their lunch boxes and post them on the family bulletin board.

Now, what words have hurt you?

I urge you to delete these words from your family's dictionary. Stop yourself from repeating them.

What you say sticks, so say the things you want them to remember, things that will build them up, give them hope, and help them have faith in themselves and feel safe and secure in your love. This will help them heal from their trauma, and it will help you heal from yours, also, because that is what choosing to love does. *It heals us.*

If you have a habit of being a bad mouth, admit it, ask for help, and then use all the tips and resources contained in this guide and all community resources available for you, including coaching and professional counseling if needed.

Looks. Our children read our faces and body language, and come to conclusions that may or may not be true about how we're feeling, especially how we are feeling about them. This is their greatest concern: how does my parent feel about me?

The simplest improvement to make is to smile more. We forget to smile because we have things on our mind and serious work to do, yet a smile reassures a child that in spite of all that, things are OK, and you are feeling good about them.

Another simple improvement is to be sure your eyes light up when you see your child. This is a gift of unspeakable value that will bring healing memories for years to come. Imagine your child saying, "I always loved the way my mother's eyes lit up when she saw me."

You might have to fake it till you make it. Love is a conscious effort—a worthy investment.

Smile more, and let your eyes twinkle when you see your children. This builds their self-esteem and sense of safety.

When you are a parent that encourages your children to talk to you—and when you listen without interrupting or judging—you have an advantage. Your children will feel heard and that they matter to you. This, in itself, is healing. Plus, you will know more about your children, which makes you better prepared to support, protect, and encourage them.

Gestures.

- Look them in the eye.
- Secret handshakes or movements that represent your unity and affection.
- Create a family tradition when it comes to special moments.

When a child is emotionally distressed, they need to be listened to with full attention, their feelings acknowledged, and their options expanded. Rather than punishing a child who is acting out and rather than denying their feelings, we need to show compassion and empathy to their suffering and look for the real underlying cause of their unwanted behavior. Parents can use the STOP method to discourage an unwanted behavior:

State the unwanted behavior.

Talk about preferred alternatives.

Offer choices.

Provide reasonable consequences.

The experts agree that when we urge children to push their feelings away, they get emotionally stuck and cannot constructively problem-solve.

I urge all of us to spend more time with our youth doing familial bonding activities. Ideally, we set aside at least thirty to sixty minutes every day doing something together, followed by individual private bonding time between parents and children.

Our communication needs to be genuine, non-judgmental, non-defensive, and non-hurried. Share feelings, fears, thoughts, actions, current stressors, safety concerns, coping skills, rules, rewards, wishes, dreams, aspirations, and ideas. There is a wealth of self-help material and in-depth training for invested parents committed to parenting at their highest possible level.

This is the most important decision any parent could ever make.

Some Dos and Don'ts

Children learn by example, and parents have more influence than they sometimes realize on their children's views, core beliefs, learning styles, and behaviors—both positively and negatively. You are their role model and primary teacher, with numerous daily opportunities to teach and demonstrate high moral standards—how to give and receive, how to be smart with finances, when to say no, the importance of teamwork, etc.

As you reconnect with your children, here are some additional dos and don'ts to keep in mind.

Do:

- Provide an environment with order, structure, and routine.
- Give allowances if you can in order to teach independence and responsibility.
- Treat each child as the unique individual they are.
- Teach children to take care of their belongings and the world around them.
- Teach them how to face obstacles.
- Teach them that setbacks are learning opportunities and not failures.
- Hold children responsible for the decisions they make and the actions they take.
- Hold them to reasonable standards.
- Explain what you require of them in a respectful language that is easy to understand.
- Help them establish healthy friendships and psychosocial support networks.
- Cooperate and work closely with their teachers.

- Allow activities as much as possible and offer a warm, consistent style of discipline that is always available.

It's certainly OK to want to know their friends, but find that balance between a heedless and a smothering parenting approach. Remember to strive to walk in their shoes and see the world from their viewpoint. Be a child for a while; that is what a role model does.

Don't:

- Break promises made to your children.
- Compare them to other children.
- Remind them of past mistakes.
- Fail to fulfill their emotional needs.
- Use only materialistic rewards.
- Focus only on shortcomings.
- Fail to hold them responsible for unacceptable behavior.
- Teach them bad habits.
- Be inflexible.
- Be excessively trusting, or suspicious.
- Scare or threaten.
- Make fun of or minimize their opinions, hopes, dreams, and aspirations.
- Shame, name, blame, or defame, especially in public.
- Administer physical, verbal, or emotional punishment.
- Wish you never had them, or make them feel like a burden.

- Give them unfair responsibilities, chores, or orders.
- Spoil them by providing privileges without them meeting reasonable requests.
- Forget to listen to their opinion as to how they want to be treated.

The time to revive our family connections is now. For in the grand scheme of life, there is no greater endeavor than that of raising a healthy and well-adjusted child. To have a solid bond with our children is indeed the most worthy of our investments.

Simple Things to Do Every Day to Love Yourself and Your Child

- Say something positive.
- Smile.
- Make eye contact.
- Say thank you.
- Believe the best of each other.
- Laugh.
- Listen—really listen.
- Breathe.
- Move.
- Eat well.
- Tell a story.
- Speak a word of praise.
- Stay safe.
- Show affection and gratitude.

Words of Hope
(collected from different sources of wisdom)

- An invested parent, through the help of a caring professional, could fill their emotional bucket and move from being discouraged to being delighted in the child and the relationship.

- In order to get children to cooperate, you do not have to threaten, blame, lecture, or command, but rather describe, give information, express your feelings, and state your expectations.

- Persistence and consistency pay, especially when combined with love and tender care.

- We have what we need to be good parents, the desire to connect and form close lasting attachment. We just need a road map and a tool kit. That is why I wrote this guide and created Project Untangled.

- It is said that teaching compassion is not easy; it is like learning a new language. We might end up with an accent, but if started early for our children it will be their native tongue. Our children deserve a better world than ours.

Notes

What do you want to remember from this section?

What help do you need?

What steps will you take to get that help?

What words of hope do you want to give to your child?

What words of hope do you want to give to yourself?

Other things you want to note:

Speak Up: It Is the Ultimate Act of Courage

Some small children seem to never stop talking, from the minute they wake up, before the alarm clock, until THEY put us to sleep.

Do we find ourselves fighting the urge to say something harsh or hurtful to our children to shut them up? I know it is not easy to always have joy in them, especially when we feel depleted and unable to keep up with their energy. But rather than reacting with anger, frustration, or dread, I invite you to admire that tender age and create delightful memories with your children before they grow up. They grow up very quickly. In their teenage years we might wish that they would just open their mouths to share something?

Children who don't feel safe, many times, lose their voice.

Have you ever lost your voice? What was that like? And what did you do to get it back?

We lose our voice for multiple reasons, most of which are organic, but there are other causes that we don't talk about much.

A physical illness like an infection, inflammation, or cancer can literally steal our ability to talk. We may then take a break from talking and give our vocal cords a chance to heal. We may use natural remedies or take medications. We may consult a speech therapist, a medical professional, or even consider a surgical procedure. In other words, **we will do whatever it takes** to regain our power to speak. But will any of us ever say, "Now that I have lost my voice, I will just forever stop talking"? The answer is most likely, "No."

Many people who experience emotional trauma metaphorically lose their voice. They may stop talking because they judge their voice as ugly, scary, or insignificant. Out of shame or the fear of being heard or unheard, they hate or hide their trauma story by turning off their voice. This is unfortunately a very common truth. Many trauma survivors do end up voiceless.

So why do we speak up when inflicted with a physical illness but become speechless when the trauma is psychological? It is fascinating, we have no issues seeking treatment for medical conditions, but when it comes to our mind, we think that suffering will somehow go away if we just ignore it. Trauma is scary, but it is here to stay, and it can happen to any of us at any time. **Silence doesn't take the trauma away; many times it makes things worse. Encourage talking. Speaking up is the ultimate act of courage.**

I now invite you to join me in writing the most important next chapter, through actions, by investing in your family and making it safe for you and them to speak up. Let us turn the ugly voices of fear and doubt to friendly ones because that is what families do. A family stands together.

I also invite you to connect and keep me updated on how you and your family are doing, working on creating the healing love you all deserve https://projectuntangled.org/

Grey skies
are just
clouds
Passing

PART 5: RESOURCES

WE ARE NOT ALONE,
there are people, ideas, groups, and resources
ready to help us heal and flourish.

Part 5: Resources

Here are some resources you may find helpful.

- https://projectuntangled.org/—an empowerment and resources site for healing from trauma.
- Raising a Secure Child: How Circle of Security Parenting Can Help You Nurture Your Child's Attachment, Emotional Resilience, and Freedom to Explore, by Kent Hoffman, Glen Cooper, and Bert Powell
- *Creative Interventions with Traumatized Children,* Second Edition (Creative Arts and Play Therapy) by Cathy A. Malchiodi and Bruce D. Perry.
- Children's Rights: https://www.unicef.org/crc/

Parent Hotlines:

- http://www.nationalparenthelpline.org/
- http://www.informationchildren.com/about-us/mission-statement/

Third-Culture Kids

- https://raseef22.com/en/culture/2017/12/09/arab-third-culture-kids-tell-us-world/
- https://en.wikipedia.org/wiki/Third_culture_kid
- https://raseef22.com/en/culture/2017/12/09/arab-third-culture-kids-tell-us-world/
- https://qz.com/1060531/between-two-cultures-what-happens-to-the-psyche-of-an-indian-child-born-and-raised-in-the-west/

Children and Trauma

- http://childtrauma.org
- https://www.youtube.com/channel/UCf4ZUgIXyxRcUNLuhimA5mA (TheChildTrauma Academy)
- https://www.nctsn.org/trauma-informed-care/families-and-trauma/introduction:
- https://www.nctsn.org/what-is-child-trauma/trauma-types/early-childhood-trauma:
- https://mom.me/kids/5249-how-traumatic-events-affect-child-development
- https://www.nctsn.org/what-is-child-trauma/trauma-types

Risks of Emergencies and Conflicts on Children

- https://en.wikipedia.org/wiki/Child

Cultural Map

- https://www.businessinsider.com/inglehart-welzel-culture-map-2014-7

Culture and Children

- http://www.tuw.edu/content/health/child-rearing-practices-different-cultures/
- http://hraf.yale.edu/a-cross-cultural-perspective-on-childhood/
- http://www.scholarpedia.org/article/Children%27s_play_and_culture
- https://www.ncbi.nlm.nih.gov/pmc/articles/PMC3433059/
- https://www.dimensionsofculture.com/2010/11/culture-and-family-dynamics/
- http://www.tuw.edu/content/health/child-rearing-practices-different-cultures/
- https://ideas.ted.com/how-cultures-around-the-world-think-about-parenting/

Trauma and Families

- https://www.nctsn.org/sites/default/files/resources//trauma_and_families_providers.pdf:

Parenting

- https://www.mother.ly/life/5-things-strong-families-have-in-common:
- https://centerforparentingeducation.org/library-of-articles/focus-parents/parents-needs/
- https://www.psychologytoday.com/us/blog/the-power-prime/201401/three-ways-raise-secure-children

Project Untangled

Project Untangled is a 501c3 organization based in Portland, Oregon. It is a comprehensive model of psychosocial care for refugees and trauma survivors founded by Harvard-trained, Libyan-American trauma expert, Dr. Omar Reda, a board-certified psychiatrist and leading professional in the field of psychological trauma.

Project Untangled uses the concepts of L.O.V.E. to assist trauma survivors in finding their voice, feeling safe, and developing self-worth—allowing them to self-forgive, gain closure, and begin their healing journey. L.O.V.E. stands for Listening, Options, Validation, and Empowerment.

We help break the cycles of trauma-related dysfunction through connection, support, education, training, safe spaces, empowerment, and the mastery of healthy coping skills.

For Professionals

If you are a mental health professional, I offer Untangled as a model of care I designed. It complements the current practices of mental health and psychosocial support.

The Untangled Model uses a trauma-sensitive, client-centered, solution-focused, future-oriented approach that covers at minimum, and within reason, the three major areas of any mental health encounter: establishing safety for all involved, addressing the underlying trauma, and reconnecting clients to their psychosocial support network.

The approach will SOOTHE clients:

Safety comes first, but hope is equally important.

Offer plenty of options.

Organize a client's experience through productive activities they choose and enjoy.

Talk about the underlying issues collaboratively (trauma work).

Help them find solutions, services, and resources.

End through empowerment, emphasizing future safety, and expanding horizons.

The Untangled model is a common-sense approach that aims to bridge gaps in the current practice of mental health, improve the status quo, fix the revolving door, prevent or reduce future dysfunction, and minimize the trans-generational transmission of trauma.

For more information, please connect with me through the Project Untangled website (https://projec-tuntangled.org/).

About the Author

Dr. Omar Reda is a board-certified psychiatrist who currently lives with his wife and three daughters in Portland, Oregon.

He graduated from Benghazi Medical School, obtained a Master's Certificate in Global Mental Health from Harvard Program in Refugee Trauma, and then finished psychiatric residency at the University of Tennessee.

Dr. Reda has served in various leadership capacities in response to humanitarian traumatic events and is actively involved in multiple youth and family healing projects nationally and internationally. He is the founder of the Oregon Muslim Medical Association (OMMA), Project Untangled, and heads many healing initiatives that help improve family bonding dynamics and empower traumatized youth.

Dr. Reda is an expert and a sought-after speaker on issues of psychological trauma; Muslim, immigrant, and refugee mental health; the Libyan revolution; and the Arab Spring. Dr. Reda himself went through the experience of fleeing his home country of Libya, seeking asylum, and living in exile.

Dr. Reda directs Project Untangled, which is more than just an organization or a model of care, but rather a global movement to heal the invisible wounds of trauma by providing survivors with a platform to find their voice, reclaim their narrative, and be empowered to thrive.

For comments or questions, or to contact Dr. Reda for speaking engagements or consultation, please contact omar@projectuntangled.org

Wishing you and your family the best of luck, and sending healing love your way.

Omar Reda, MD

Portland, Oregon, USA

2019

Dedication

To my beloved parents, thank you for everything you have done for me. May God reward you with the highest heaven, and help me make you proud. Mom, you are never gone. You will always be in my heart and thoughts. I miss you dearly, but I know that you are watching over me.

To my beautiful wife, Nura, and our three precious girls, thank you for sticking with me through the good and bad times. May God help me be a better husband and father.

To all the deliberate parents and caregivers out there, thank you for trying to make the world a better place by investing in your families. Thank you for being part of the solution.

And most importantly, to all the young souls suffering in silence, know that you are not alone. Thank you for your courage. I pray that your wounds are healed soon, and that you untangle to continue your journey of safety, hope, recovery, and prosperity.

Acknowledgments

I would like to thank God for giving me the strength to finish this writing, and I ask Him to give me the courage to see this dream come true by making Project Untangled a reality through healing and empowering our youth and their families and caregivers worldwide.

I would like to thank my parents for giving me a wonderful childhood. To mom, my best friend, who I recently lost, I feel your warm beloved presence around me at all times.

Also, I would like to thank my wife who stands by my side as we try to make the childhood of our three girls a happy one.

Thank you Jan Black, Doreen Dodgen-Magee, Paul Salerno, Tim Gilman, and Eric Muhr for believing in me and helping with editing and publishing my books. You represent humanity at its best.

None of this would be possible without the support of my family and friends, the tireless work of many volunteers, and without the heart-filled sharing of hope and healing by many trauma survivors who enriched my life and made me not only a better physician but a better human as well.

We can untangle the web of trauma together.

CPSIA information can be obtained
at www.ICGtesting.com
Printed in the USA
BVHW062029250122
627130BV00004B/105

9 781594 980596